WHEN

WHEN

Baron Wormser

Winner of the 1996
Kathryn A. Morton Prize in Poetry
Selected by Alice Fulton

Sarabande Books
LOUISVILLE, KENTUCKY

Managing Editor
Sarabande Books, Inc.
2234 Dundee Road, Suite 200
Louisville, KY 40205

LIBRARY OF CONGRESS CATALOGING-IN-PUBLICATION DATA

Wormser, Baron.
     When : poems / by Baron Wormser. — 1st ed.
          p. cm.
     ISBN 1-889330-03-5 (cloth : alk. paper). — ISBN 1-889330-04-3
(paper : alk. paper)
     I. Title
PS3573.0693W46   1997
811' .54—dc20   96-44929
                                                             CIP

Cover Painting: *Man in Charge,* by Wendy Kindred. Reproduced with the kind permission of the artist.

Cover and text design by Charles Casey Martin.

Manufactured in the United States of America.
This book is printed on acid-free paper.

Sarabande Books is a nonprofit literary organization.

For Tom Hart

Contents

Foreword

"Fashion fades, only style remains," Coco Chanel observed. Poetry, like couture, is subject to trends of chic. I'm happy to say that Baron Wormser's poems are not fashion victims. His work is permeated by a linguistic singularity that amounts to style: an ongoing poetic engagement untouched by poetic trends.

When is Wormser's fourth book. His earlier volumes—*The White Words, Good Trembling, Atoms, Soul Music, and Other Poems*—are characterized by a moral intelligence that recognizes the personal and political intertwinings of American culture. In *When,* it seems to me that Wormser has gentled his earnestness while retaining his distinctive tone. I found myself convinced by the poems' integrity and maturity as I read and reread. By invoking integrity, I mean to praise a relation to language and issues that is iconoclastic rather than imitative, that tries to go deeper rather than to please—for Wormser isn't a pleaser. He doesn't succumb to the tonal preciousness and lyric prettiness, the emotional gush and self-dramatization that characterize much contemporary poetry. It's not that his poetry is unfeeling, but that his work lets me detect "out of the boisterous muddle /Of feeling a glimmer of discipline...." ("Sister Angela")

Feeling without discipline is bathos; discipline without feeling is formula. When Wormser writes of suffering, he avoids solipsism and self-pity by looking to the pain of others. Yet he has absorbed the external to such a degree that his renditions of the nonself are, obliquely, songs of himself. In "Dramatis Personae," for instance, an imaginative boy plays the parts of literary characters and friends to the bewilderment of his pragmatic father. Like that boy, Wormser assumes otherness so convincingly that I suspect him of being the stockbroker or senior citizen he creates. He writes from that rare spiritual terrain where life responds to life, thinking beyond his own circumstance toward that of a man who was gay in the closet of the 1950s; a black woman working as a white family's maid; farmers who "go crazy slowly;" cows raised for slaughter; a male prostitute. These encounters with alterity reveal a world view that is rigorous without being callous, tough-minded without being bitter. Rather than cherubic innocents, for instance, the young patients in his "Children's Ward" are stoical, resigned, and at times, mean-spirited. They are, as another Wormser poem would have it, "incurably human."

> The TV gambols but the beds are brisk and
> Neat as lined paper or utopian cities.
> If you make enough motions you might go home.
> You lecture your tumors and talk to your bones.
> It's work to stare at the wincing lights—
> A mirror might leap at you, a nurse.
> It's work to eat, to search out your voice,
> To smile at the smiles, to sleep when it's night.

> Everyone gets tired so fast. "Last century," the Princess
> Says to Short Legs, "we'd all be dead.
> We'd all be sleeping the everlasting sleep.
> We'd never know what it's like to be even as old
> As ten is. We'd be mummies, creeps..."

The honesty of the poems is rare. By honesty, I don't mean confession or adherence to autobiographical facts. There is a revelation beyond the diaristic, a rectitude that excavates hard truths—truths that are hard on the poet, that is. When Wormser writes of being seventeen and collecting rents with a slumlord, both the poet-speaker and his employer are implicated in "this life / Which disfigures our years." ("Rent") "Fans," a poem that remembers the deaths of Janis Joplin and Jimi Hendrix, neither hides behind protective irony nor valorizes the rock stars.

x

I played their records
And felt again how they turned terror into
    a good time:
He was screechingly wry, she was throbbingly kind.
Like the GIs they had told us about in school
These people died so
Others could live—
    but we could have lived if they had lived.

Biographical explorations of famous people have become a popular poetic genre over the last twenty-five years. Rather than studying up on Joan of Arc or Van Gogh and regurgitating his learning, however, Wormser imagines those who became a part of history without becoming visible: "Simon Turetzky Who Died at Dachau" and "Beethoven's Maid." His poems tend to be tales of "friendly strangers": Tricia LeClair, who "liked to dab perfume all / Over her body, places that were (as she later/ Put it) 'out of the way.' " Raymond, who leaves a bequest of notebooks filled with weather because "The feeling of being present each day was—/ When you got right down to it— lordly." He also considers subtle misfits on the outskirts of acceptability: the shoplifter who steals film yet doesn't own a camera, the man who drives 400 miles a week with no destination in search of absolution. Failure is one of Wormser's subjects. Yet rather than judge individual players, the poems appraise the cultures we create together. *When* presents people affected by particular epochs, and this acknowledgment of temporal context is forgiving. "It's a Party (1959)," Wormser's evocation of suburbia, has the caustic sweetness and canny details of a John Cheever story.

The rhododendron is happy. Its aloof yet sexual
    blossoms glimmer in the cool April moonlight.
The pebbles in the driveway croon very softly.
The Negro ceramic jockey, which toward the end of the next
    decade the children who are now asleep in

their Snuggy-Pooh pajamas will unceremoniously
smash as a honky, racist artifact, extends an arm
of welcome.

An unabashedly American poet, Wormser has a sense of place which
extends beyond suburbia to missile silos, Las Vegas, housing projects,
and traffic on the beltways. He has written a gently splendid poem of
retirement country—Arizona, Florida, the Farm, the Home.

This is no place to die—
And that is why we are all here.
Our resentments against our old lives
Dwindle mercifully. I no longer
Wake up wishing to choke that
Swindling two-timer Sternblatt.
This is what America calls "contemplative,"
Where you find the courage perhaps
To realize you never grasped what it was
You so diligently and lengthily did.

This "American Poem of the Senior Citizenry," like many others in
the collection, shows humor in the face of what cannot be changed,
and bravery under duress. The sobriety of Wormser's tonal shadings
reminds me, at times, of W.H. Auden and of Marianne Moore.
"Bemusement was the better part of sanity…" he writes at the open-
ing of "Elegy for a Detective," going on to note that "much-praised
love was / Our most condign misunderstanding, / The hurtling of
hope into the gasps of flesh." The ghost of Auden also shimmers
through Wormser's formal, rhymed poems. Metered poems are no
longer in vogue, the New Formalist contrivance of the eighties having
died an uncontrived death. Wormser, however, was not a New For-
malist then, and he is not a subscriber to any head-turning school of
poetics today. I suspect he writes the kind of work he would like to
read. Structurally, his poems oscillate in focal length, moving in for

concrete close-ups and retreating for abstract reflections voiced as declaratives. His gift for aphorisms puts me in mind of Moore's potent definitions. "Reduction was the imp of genius...", he begins "Comics." Or consider the first sentence of this meditation on aesthetics and the American soul:

> Poetry is the logic beyond reason. That's what keeps you reading
> all these twitchy nights. Inside the tread of days and years
> there's a labyrinth. On its walls are candles of words. They
> bruise the illimitable shadows. You pull the car off the road
> and get out. There's a smooth, taut breeze. You shiver. Back
> in the city another kid is eating the trigger. ("Poems")

The register downshifts from high lyric to colloquial eloquence as the poem wanders from Rilke to handguns. Wormser has a fine ear, and vocabulary is an important component of his scrupulous—and rather sumptuous—style. Today's generic poem depends upon a lexicon so limited and exhausted by overuse as to constitute poetic diction. (I'd rather have an ecstatic nosebleed than submit to one more lyric-narrative decorated with "angels" and "desire.") Given this simplistic predilection, it's refreshing to find Baron Wormser using the full range of the language in poems that resurrect words like "feckless," and don't shy away from "motherfucker." Words both well-chosen and unlikely are embedded like flecks of musk and phosphorous within the fiber of the lines, infusing them with aroma and glow: "sun" is modified by "ardent;" "music" by "stoic;" "consolations" by "God's." ("Pikesville")

"Pikesville," and several other poems, depict Jewish-American culture, quietly invoking the shadow of anti-Semitism to comment acerbically on human nature when it becomes what the waiters of "Rudinsky's, 1953" called "the human disgrace." Wormser worries about cruelty—whether it takes the shape of a nuclear arsenal or troops who rape and kill a twelve-year-old girl. He writes of violence and beauty without conflating the two. Unlike much poetry of conscience, his work does not ask us to admire the poet's sensitivity. When he says "I want to be a member of / The gouging, tie-loosed, bourbon-gulping choir." or "I want to believe in the effervescence / Of ignorance...", I both believe and disbelieve him. He wants respite from the vigilance of ethics, yet his mindfulness keeps worrying the world into poetry.

His largest concern is the interconnectedness of What-Is: "Every moment / is expressive and it flows into you like some grand river out / West. Your soul's a canyon. And their souls too." ("Poems") In "A Quiet Life," the simple act of eating an egg is shown to depend upon a complex network of community and causality: "There must be gas and a stove, / the gas requires pipelines, mastodon drills, / banks that dispense the lozenge of capital." Eating an egg, when you think about it, illustrates the symbiosis of the personal and political.

> It should be quiet
> when one eats an egg. No political hoodlums
> knocking down doors, no lieutenants who are
> ticked off at their scheming girlfriends and
> take it out on you, no dictators
> posing as tribunes.
> It should be quiet, so quiet you can hear
> the chicken, a creature usually mocked as a type
> of fool, a cluck chained to the chore of her body.
> Listen, she is there, pecking at a bit of grain
> that came from nowhere.

From nowhere? Stanza by stanza the poem has shown the intricate production of the stove, pot, water, salt, and political peace required for the eating of an egg. According to this dialectic, grain comes, not "from nowhere," but from seed, soil, tractors, pesticides, agribiz and human toil. Yet the chicken-and-egg riddle is a recursive structure. It draws us back along multiplying chains of causality in search of a First Cause: the unattainable origin named "God," the nowhere from which

"All" issues. As it builds toward closure, this last lovely koan of a poem ventures beyond linguistic endowments to question the quiet of quietude, the end of finitude. "A Quiet Life"—and other works in the collection—have a ceiling higher, a depth lower, and a breadth wider than their manifest dimensions. Resistant to summary, they dilate in mind.

Alice Fulton
Ypsilanti, Michigan
July, 1996

WHEN

Somerset County

The log-crammed trucks smash the yielding air,
Whine like leviathan gnats.
Last week a trucker died at the wheel
On the way home from the mill.
He fell asleep. Or did he wake before?
The wreck looked like a freighter run aground.

One January day, a pulpwood driver tells me,
He skidded the better part of a quarter-mile
Toward a stopped school bus.
He played the brake and gears
Like the valves of a trumpet, soft and hard.
And he said he saw himself as a boy:
"About eight-years-old—
You forget that stuff."

If summer is the sovereign remedy,
The pure swat of northern heat,
Its pleasure lies in ineffability
The true green that governs growing things
But is bound to retreat,
Bound to turn sullen and spare,
Bound to wait wordlessly in the spell of winter.
Patience was never a human virtue
And never will be.

At the end of August the air is so clear and light
A body could levitate,
Fly off without benefit of preacher or motor,
Shedding the responsible wrenches, the keys.
That's a fantasy—not a word I hear often,
If ever.

Hard knowledge wants a sharp edge.
A pile of metal filings from lathe or saw is swept

To the floor or ground and forgotten,
The power of work needing that precision
And that waste.

Listening to a Baseball Game

The smothering heat of a July night
Squats in a second-floor bedroom
And doesn't move despite the desk fan's
Peaceful whir and simulate breeze.
A boy lies on the sheets and reads
A *Life* magazine which holds
The proper shadow of attention
While he listens to the ballgame
Being played in Kansas City.
He sees it happen and imagines it—
The same thing really. A car swings

Down Maple Street, a hinge complains.
Moths move toward decipherable light
But are stopped by screens. The boy's done
Reading and lies there beside the lamp,
His hands folded beneath his head.
He knows that comfort is rarely pure.
He listens and lets his feelings glide
With each intent description.
He follows a probable dream
As the night sways with outcomes
In houses and rooms and far away.

(for Charles Baxter)

Poems

In July, under the sign of Cancer when Vega climaxes,
it's small firearms time. A modest piece carries a strong
message. At several thousand feet, doors splinter like
kindling. Up close, to a person, it's a splatter.
People are rivers. They're dammed-up rivers.

The sound's so short, it's like a comma, not even
an exclamation mark. It's a high, groaning pop.

Uncle Ed shows me his complete arsenal—at least fifteen
weapons of various calibers. "An armed citizenry is the best
defense against tyranny." He says that to me. He got
laid off two years short of retirement. He security guards
for two bucks over minimum wage. "It's not a cop, but it's
not not a cop," he says over Aunt Minna's thick coffee.

No one much recognizes a name in a newspaper, a shooting name—
no one's looking at a paper for that knowledge—
unless maybe you're a student teacher for a semester in
the city and you know that it's that kid, Rinaldo. He liked
to do long division. One day he told you not to interrupt
him with your foolishness. He was learning something. He was
about a couple of months over eleven.

You're up late reading Rilke. The poems drift like swans
on a rippling pond. Later you're in the car on the way to
the Cape. There's no traffic and it's quiet as it can be in
the machine. Outside it's still hot, the air sticky and thick.
You catch yourself waiting for a sound, a siren, the trumpet
of someone else's doom. "...*hinter tausend Stäben keine Welt*":
you turn off the a.c.

Poetry is the logic beyond reason. That's what keeps you reading
all these twitchy nights. Inside the tread of days and years

there's a labyrinth. On its walls are candles of words. They
bruise the illimitable shadows. You pull the car off the road
and get out. There's a smooth, taut breeze. You shiver. Back
in the city another kid is eating the trigger.

In the lockup someone's shouting "motherfucker" fairly loudly
but no one's interested. In your room it's deep in the middle
of the night and you're sleeping. You're dreaming. You see so
many faces each day in the subway, on the streets. Every moment
is expressive and it flows into you like some grand river out
West. Your soul's a canyon. And their souls too.

For D.R., Dead of AIDS at Age 25

The drift that plunges down tendriled roots
Hardening what is soft, drawling
Hideous vagaries is impossibly earned.

You mustn't do what you mustn't do:
The coyness of possible days, the statuesque law
Of permissible passion, is suitably explained.

In the new Bible thorns are random,
Hope is a cinder, the judgment grotesque.
There are too many impulses and too many tests.

The body has failed at love before but not like this.
The stem of life has been split.
Beauty like paper ash

And the privilege of forgetfulness buried
In another kingdom in another reign
In a world before pain.

American Poem of the Senior Citizenry

I. Arizona

The lungers stick together, as do
The arthritic, the lame, and those
Who are mysteriously whole.
Everyone protests his or her vigor
While comparing coughs and cures,
Telephone calls from successful children.
Immaculate cells litter the landscape
Where lizards breed and gods appeared
Out of the weatherless sky.
Immaculate lawns invoke the peace
Of pebbles, light posts, asphalt.
Even the ambulances are quiet.
If life repeats the same anecdote,
One must be thankful for blessed tedium.
Something else could happen, something
Headshaking, dizzy, abrupt.
Everyone celebrates birthdays with
The passion of partying children:
Another hot dog, feigned distress,
And that old singsong the wavering voices
Never want to let go.

II. Florida

Steinberg,
                    the most garish philosophies prosper
In this place. Every other widow is
A cardsharping, Zionist, diet-mystic.
The ones in-between follow the Stock
Market the way we rooted for

The Polo Grounds Giants.
Young naked bodies are everywhere.
Tribes of them bow down before
The sun like new-age Mayans.
The corned beef though is good
And there is condoed culture:
Mozart in Miami, chess games
That placate eternity,
Lending libraries as eager to
Dispense murder mysteries as history.
This is no place to die—
And that is why we are all here.
Our resentments against our old lives
Dwindle mercifully. I no longer
Wake up wishing to choke that
Swindling two-timer Sternblatt.
This is what America calls "contemplative,"
Where you find the courage perhaps
To realize you never grasped what it was
You so diligently and lengthily did.
Red sails in the sunset, Steinberg,
And dividend checks in the mail.

III. Farm

Not many people know as much about
Silence as a farmwife does.
She has the quiet keys.
She could be a cat.
Solitary labor, Ralph used to call it.
He worked and worked, I worked and worked.
The children grew like trees.
How many times I looked out that kitchen

Window at games of ball, rain, a balky heifer.
It was all gone even as I looked,
And I understood that.
People fear the land.
They gather in cities, and they talk,
Always talking like on the damn TV.
This country doesn't know enough to shut up.
You can be too strong, of course, too silent,
But that's the earth's element.
It's empty here and it was
And I hope it always will be.

IV. The Home

Dosage charts phantasms of pain
The doctor from some foreign country
The teenage girls who take away the bedpans

One morning sure begins to look like another

The phenomenal cheerfulness
As relentless as the body

No summary will do

Playing hearts and bingo
Cheating scrupulously

The stages between life and death

As when a tree dies or a soul must
Make a perilous journey
Traveling through jello catheters pills

Invisible to the workaday eye

Buttoning buttons very carefully

Weeping old-fashioned rich weeping
Over abandonments illusions
The mirth of such friendly strangers

Dramatis Personae (1957)

If I looked down through the good-sized cracks
Between the hayloft's floor boards,
I could see my father querying the car engine
While skinning his knuckles, discarding cigarette ash

And occasionally lifting his head to the voice
In the loft that was carefully mimicking
A range (both male and female) of TV celebrities,
Famous literary characters—Crusoe, Jane Eyre,

And most winningly, I thought, the brazen Huck Finn—
Plus politicos, athletes (Splendid Ted),
And every boy and girl in the East Wain sixth grade.
I bounded around appropriately and enjoyed best

The moments when fantasies crossed, when Jane Whittemore,
Who ate five candy bars a day and could whistle through
Her front teeth, met General Ulysses S. Grant.
My father had a habit of dropping wrenches

Into inaccessible places. He'd pause and look about him,
Reach for a Lucky and say something to himself
In a voice so low it seemed he himself couldn't hear it.
It wasn't a secret though. He didn't seem to have

Any of those. He'd look up and I knew he was wondering
Where in tarnation he'd gotten such a boy.
When he dimmed the light downstairs, he'd always say,
"Now, don't you forget to come in."

(for Sandy Phippen)

Tricia LeClair

Striding manfully up the front walk
I saw Tricia LeClair looking at me
Through her bedroom window—blooming
Moonface and eager brown eyes.
Her mother spoke to me in a tone

She saved for salesmen, infants, and dogs.
I could smell Tricia in the next room:
She liked to dab perfume all
Over her body, places that were (as she later
Put it) "out of the way." I gulped too happily

And wondered where she got such tiny feet.
Impatient and overwhelmed, we tackled one another
A half-mile away. Even when we did it again
Things went too fast. Sliding into great glimmers,
So warm we couldn't tell our flesh from

Our thoughts, we whizzed past every prior moment
And when we tottered up to her porch light
At two before the curfew of midnight
We tried to count fireflies, our heartbeats,
And the not improbable stars.

Rudinsky's, 1953

In the back of my grandfather's delicatessen
The waiters talked about the bad things.
Dropping dishes, that was more than bad,
It was a curse, a shame on the profession.
That's what they called it, a profession.
Nowadays that means sitting through college
But there was a lot to it—you had to be swift
And deft, you had to be strong, you had to be patient,
You had to be calm. Lots of qualities.

Like monkeys, diners did all sorts of things.
They weren't just there to eat. The families
Maybe but the couples had other thoughts.
But the bad things—slipping was a bad thing,
Not adding up a check correctly, setting
The wrong dish down, forgetting to pour the water.
The waiters watched for each other and looked out for each other.
They were mothers and brothers to each other.

Have you ever been on your legs for ten hours straight?
Do it for thirty years and we'll talk about it.

The waiters knew everything there was to know
About the human disgrace (as they called it).
To keep their wits alert they bet on the size
Of a tip before a party sat down. They bet
On how many drinks, which desserts, sugar in
The coffee, how many trips to the can.
Clothes, eyes, manners, speech:
Everything was a fact and a hint—
One day or another everything had happened.
Farters, no-tippers, complainers,
Drunks, check-skippers, glass-breakers.
It was a reputable place but people were
Going to be people no matter where they were.

Women stuffed pickles in their pocketbooks,
Men grabbed handfuls of toothpicks.
The worst thing was a lady making eyes at you.
Only misery could come of that. One night
A fellow threw a plate of blintzes at a waiter,
"Bothering my girl, you lousy Jew."
They shook their heads and made disgusted faces.

You could know everything, that was the funny part,
But it didn't help. As in a dream you saw
It before it was going to happen but still it happened.
Like the Nazis or rain or when you go to get
The last piece of cheesecake and it's not there.

Single-Life Blues

People say to be good to yourself
Oh people say to be good to yourself
I'd rather be good with someone else

I'm living with no ring on my left hand
Oh I'm living with no ring on my left hand
You can't make much music in a one-man band

If I got a phone call I'd kiss that machine
Oh if I got a phone call I'd kiss that machine
Because a voice does better than a dream

I think about leaving this miserable town
Oh I think about leaving this miserable town
But my heart has got used to this unhappy ground

I must have stepped on an evil-days crack
Oh I must have stepped on an evil-days crack
A few more of those steps and I won't come back

Pikesville

Beside each semi-regal home, surrounded by
    slatted fence and yews, an air conditioner
    growls consolingly.
A deep summer night lolls overhead, soft
    and ruminant.
It is late.
Human kernels sleep inside their huge square footage;
    their dreams shuffle the deck of longing.
I'm up, undrugged, twenty, reading Baudelaire
    in French, a poet whom I adore but whose taste
    for sin I do not understand.
I wander through his Paris of syphilis and gaslights,
    the modern and medieval grotesque.

This suburb is an elective ghetto;
    each split-level upholds the striving star of Jews
    who lived through the nickels and dimes of
    the Depression to buy autos, shrubs, pedigreed dogs,
    swimming pools, and sit beneath the ardent sun on
    potted patios.
I go for a walk on the macadam streets.
A tassel of a breeze strums the ornamental trees.
I'm crazy to touch someone, anyone.

I'm in that Paris; my sneakered feet make little slaps.
I pull out a silk handkerchief.
Voices from doorways, the dragoons of pleasure.
I stare up at a creamy half-moon.
My fingers ache.

The guardian machines click and pulse, a stoic music.
Precipitously I stroll past
    graydark houses, a synagogue, carports.
The Jews of Paris shift in their sleep, envisioning
    the calm wealth of God's consolations.

It's a Party (1959)

The rhododendron is happy. Its aloof yet sexual
    blossoms glimmer in the cool April moonlight.
The pebbles in the driveway croon very softly.
The Negro ceramic jockey, which toward the end of the next
    decade the children who are now asleep in
    their Snuggy-Pooh pajamas will unceremoniously
    smash as a honky, racist artifact, extends an arm
    of welcome.
People drink, eat, and talk elaborately:
    It's the death of Charlie Parker
    A grandma who swims laps at the Y each day
    Crabcakes
    Zoning bribes
    Sartre's existential pride.
If everyone is aware of everyone else,
    everyone is unconcerned too.
The halftones of sex
    craft a jauntily steamy mood
    of nods and titters, long and longer looks.
It's
Eric Dolphy
Trane
Charles Mingus.
No one is peeved or grumpy,
    no one complains how life wronged him or her,
    no one bitches about how this was not
    the planet he or she ordered.
It's
Life in the big adrenaline city
Life in shack-roof, deputy-sheriff Mississippi
Life in a Nash Rambler, looking out
    windows at oblivious trees.

Winks and shrugs as soft as rayon.
People muse and kiss.

Someone in black pants is lying on his back.
Someone is thumbing through a book from the big bookcase.
Someone is downing other people's drinks:
    bourbon, Scotch, sloe gin.
There's nothing like reading Proust when you're drunk.
There's nothing like touching someone's skin
    you've wanted to touch for hours.
There's nothing like delivering an enlightened opinion
    and laughing at yourself seconds later
    for being so stiflingly correct.

Someone hoots like a well-bred owl.
Someone flings peanuts into his mouth.
Someone yawns fiercely
    as the jazz, the lofty gritty searching
    elegantly churning jazz
    the sympathetic overheard genius plays on.

Swayed

A boy, I marked a circle around a tree,
A hobbling line on a tethered, winter's day.
I meant to cordon infinity;
I meant to guard what I could not say

And felt obscurely. A conjuring clattering stick
In my right hand I struck at horizons
And heights. I would perform a human trick,
One that answered the wan, dying sun

In the rose-hazed west. That first thrilling chill
Of death in the late afternoon, the tiny power
That tastes extinction like snow in the still
Air and rejoices that the final hour

Is far off, unknown. I was blood-magic
And swayed beneath the ash tree like a cantor,
Intoning nubs of sounds, gesturing with quick
Unpracticed jerks. Crazy no doubt or

Something simpler. I see the boy alert
In near darkness, head back to see the sky—
A veil laid over an ancient earth,
The truest irrelevant guide.

Simon Turetzky Who Died at Dachau

If everyone had heard of Simon Turetzky,
It wasn't on account of some perfected quirk
As might have sauced a Berlin novel,
A man of margins and tantrums, without a name,
A feverish cipher, but something of the opposite—
Solid, godly but shrewd, a lumber dealer,
Benefactor, a man who did not shrink from a jest,
Who announced his appetites and acted,
Whose years added up to more than numbers.
He spoke at times too much but listened also.
When he heard of the place in the East to where
He'd be sent by them, of birds and wheat there,
He laughed a deep dire laugh and screwed
His eyes as if to see around a corner.
There were birds and wheat already here, even fish
That appeared each spring after fresh spring.
They were deaf and chose to stay in their
Anointed places. Simon knew that God knew this.
Simon was deaf too: the murdered sounds in the shul
Could not be heard, his horse could not be heard,
His children who asked such childish questions,
The sawmill could not be heard and yet
He listened as he had always listened. It was sad
But ridiculous and he asked himself at night
In the soundless house why he couldn't hear.
It was only when he walked along the stream
That cut through the little grove of poplars that
He knew that whatever happened in these countries
And counties and courtyards, God heard, God heard.

Mark Rothko, 1903–1970

Immaterial subject matter
Imperfect essences
Sang to him as he soliloquized
Our metaphysical flesh.
He flailed the arts of likeliness.

The tragedy of headlines
Ecstatic mass salutes
Celebrated more misrule.
He shook the hopeful,
Darkened spear of myth.

The shoppers stood on 14th Street
Leering despondently:
Access of feeling
Became a complaint.
He held for a new lament:

Not bodies but forms, equivocally tense,
Ragged and poised, testing proximity,
Haggardly and grandly present because
Within the human ligature
Dramas churned, the shapes

That first-time lovers descried
In hot tenderness, the stolid chills
Of rage and repose. Soul soul soul.
The paint bled rectangularly. Duress smiled—
Our madonna of modern signs.

Diary of an Ant

Because I never definitively sit
I am the object of complacent wit,
My busy aptitudes the core of jests
About the paths of small-mindedness.

Easy enough to comment on the ways
Of those who must earn each grudging day.
Be warned: a still life is a painterly fib;
Decay is matter's fate, its poses are glib.

Few understand how the sober may be avid.
To seize a bit of rough-hewn prey that's hid
Beneath a blade, then face the perils of terrain
Indifferent to exertion, time and pain—

Few understand. Explaining does no good.
You have to feel your own way out of the woods,
Feel the snap of tension and intent
As you recoup what might have been misspent.

Freedom's heroic stance is always awry
To my mute, deterministic eye.
The service of instinct is dignity enough:
The prudent body is improvident stuff.

Only yesterday I tugged wholeheartedly
At a green bug twice the size of me
When out of the sky appeared that wretched shape
Whose sole effect is to smash, mar, efface

Whatever lurks beneath its massy breadth.
Did wariness ever deflect the ace of death?
I shouldered on, the tally of missteps.
I live to write this down and not to guess.

Who St. Augustine Was

He's trying to tell his seventh-period class
About the fourth century A.D. and
Who St. Augustine was
And Jeanie Holzapple who's reading
A *Soap Opera Digest* snugged inside her textbook
(He confiscates one every now and then to keep
Her alert) looks up at the clock and on the way
Back to her 'zine gazes as if she were staring
At the ground from an airplane window
At twenty thousand feet:
"What is that?" her eyes say, "What is that?"

After seventeen years of World History, Mr. Pfeiffer
Knows indifference. He's been there and if
Most of his compadres have retreated
Into the chirpy glimmer of videocation
He still likes to slug it out in real time
Even if it's mud most days,
Sheer bored and bruised adolescent gumbo.

So he asks if anyone's wished someone else
Had dropped dead in the past week,
And Tony Campbell has his hand up fast
And says, "Yeah, you!" before Pfeiffer can even call
His name and everyone laughs because if he were gone
Maybe seventh period would disappear too.

After a certain number of furtive looks, more hands
Go up until most of the class has them up—
Some defiant, some abashed, some grim and
He tells them they're all depraved and
St. Augustine knew they were depraved and that's
Why all high schools have assistant principals
Because of the ungovernable wickedness in everyone.
St. Augustine had their number.

"But I'm not bad," says Shelly Grossman
Who didn't raise her hand, and everyone looks at her
And he sees some strong smirks appear on some faces.
"Now who's a Donatist and who's Augustinian?" he asks
While moving toward the blackboard and then he's singing,
"You're no good, you're no good, you're no good,"
As he begins writing words and drawing arrows
Which brings Jeanie out of her *Digest*
Because his voice is atrocious
And twenty-three minutes go by in contorted, excited
Conversation about the nature of people and God.

That's when the bell rings and they all let go of their
Imagining. Pfeiffer goes over to the window and breathes
Deeply. The bad air feels good, the silence has wings.

Children's Ward

Accident Face tells Breathless to let go,
It's not her toy, it's his. She drops the plastic gun
And stings him with her X-ray eyes.
He might be a bug or a painting. "Oh, Monster Boy,"
She hisses, "Halloween is history.
You don't need a mask." Her skull tilts back.
Her laugh is amusement and nonchalant fright.

Two baldies are wheeled in from chemo.
Empty Heart has messed himself and is whining.
"But he's always whining," the Princess of Pain
Explains to her rag doll. "He likes to whine."
Winter light scouts the dirty windows.
Mourning doves moan. There's a sky.

The TV gambols but the beds are brisk and
Neat as lined paper or utopian cities.
If you make enough motions you might go home.
You lecture your tumors and talk to your bones.
It's work to stare at the wincing lights—
A mirror might leap at you, a nurse.
It's work to eat, to search out your voice,
To smile at the smiles, to sleep when it's night.

Everyone gets tired so fast. "Last century," the Princess
Says to Short Legs, "we'd all be dead.
We'd all be sleeping the everlasting sleep.
We'd never know what it's like to be even as old
As ten is. We'd be mummies, creeps..."

Practice makes tenacity perfect, hope shrieks more than
It sighs. Somewhere, children are not thinking.
"But we," the Princess says, "must live in this story."

Young Ahab

Your typical adolescent innocent-decadent,
Ahab ran off at age fifteen
Determined to mitigate his virginity
And fly the flag of candor. Strange seas.
Patterns of senselessness witnessed by men

And women who claimed to elude
The damnable rules. Crockery, kittens, knives—
All thrown at him. Venial sins woven
Of mysteries. Curses on his head,
Evasions, the ruminations born of rum.

To and fro men and women go on these waters:
Falling off masts, crushed by metals,
Mutilated and drowned. Limbs are chances.

No light in the gray, foggy mornings,
The cold spray flung like an insult.
Weak faces of men and women groveling,
Stamping on the same speck of earth.
The depths of seas are the prodigal

Taunts of death bearing up
Little worlds that are baubles.
Men and women are answering God
With the blunt vigor of wooden creeds
And brave ships. Maddened love.

Sonnet

When the troops don't find the trade union
Leader at home (some intelligence misconstrued),
They swear and look for someone else to ruin:
A shrieking girl of twelve will have to do.
They stuff her mouth with gloves; they tear her sex
Like cellophane; they force her anus, then beat
Her skull with the butt of a pistol until flecks
Of bone obtrude. Now, they have not been cheated.

They light machine-rolled cigarettes and go.
When next evening the priest arrives, he smells
The smoke of candles. His breath stalls but after slow,
Steep seconds it returns, the knell
Of life. *If then he fell he might not rise.*
He speaks—so that all that is human might die.

On the Bus to Houston

Smashing sticks of gum till her jaw smarts,
Looking for something out there to look at,

Some scenery while the guy beside her
Keeps stretching his mouth but says nothing.

He gives off a crazy-type vibe: he could
Lose it any minute and not know it.

He is going to touch her, she knows it.
She's sat on more than one daddy's knee

And she doesn't want the littlest touch of those hands.
The book in her lap stays shut—a mystery,

People talk to each other, kill each other;
It makes a kind of twisted sense.

She's wearing black though no one in her life has died.
It's her traveling dress; it keeps people quiet.

In a pale, taunting way she's pretty:
As if that mattered, as if there were

An honest man to whom she could say
That her beauty has been a joke.

The guy is going to fall asleep.
He looks sort of dog-like sweet.

He isn't though. She's too educated
About the wrong things. Somewhere in books,

Her twin is alive. She's not better
Or worse. What she is, is clear,

As if someone cleaned a body, cleaned
It till it glowed like nobody's dream.

Beethoven's Maid

A spare, vigorous woman with crinkly hair
The color of straw,
She possessed a notable recipe for
Poppyseed rolls.

No stove could subdue her.
An altogether responsible, upright woman,
She mistrusted children, horses and love.
Also geniuses

Though at first she did not know what one was.
She knew temperament and anger
But not to be looked at as if she were not there—
That was new.

"He has just woken up—always,"
She told a friend or, "He never goes to sleep.
He makes strange sounds as if
Suffocating or vomiting air."

She heard the ever-larger pianos erupt
Like steam then subside to a sigh
Though what startled her most was not
The musician so much as

The lords and ladies who fawned over
A little, disheveled man. "He is inspired,
A creator," a gentleman gushed to her
As if that vein of purple feeling

Had not existed before.
November rain pattered on the roof;
Flame sang in the stove.
She preferred what endured.

Cow Symphony

Ovals of crushed September stubble
Where the weight has rested quilt the field.
The ambling toward the block of salt,

The algae-mouthed pond, tree shade
Or blade, stalk, leaf, kernel,
Or what seems movement for the sake

Of movement, purity of motive uncommonly
Encountered. Whimsical tonnage
Pissing and shitting unfugitively.

Beautiful globular eyes, demure tails,
Rough colors—browns Cezanne loved,
Always applied variously to

Each canvas of hoofed being.
Stomachs that cannot be seen.
Calves frolic, kindled, surging

With breath, blood, breeze, bodyness—
Trying out gravity, greeting ground.
Molten bellows, squeals, pacific grunts,

Cloppings, settling sighs, and fearful
Stubborn bovine bleats when the truck
Comes to collar what seemed so hugely free.

(for Janet)

Comics

Reduction was the imp of genius as
These panels of heroes, sages, and dolts held me
Handily, the weight of my childhood dispersed.

Deathlessness, of course, and agelessness
Without the salt of self-awareness, an intent
Dumbness that seemed to free the actors
For flights of more rapturous immediacy.
Their legs not legs but the efficacy of legs,
Their bodies assuming vegetable shapes,

Thin and lumpy though volatile, as when
Bullets disgorged inner matter with
A smooth, electric thrust.

Adventures were incidents; sallies contained
The ragged marrow of philosophy,
And names were bluntly abject:

No "Misters" here.
                    Decades later
The lure remains as I pause before the scores.
Some other hand is drawing Jug and Spider Man

And I remark it in a connoisseur's instant:
The outlines aren't the same. I try to feel
Betrayed but fail: their ministrations cannot change.

Vegas: the Urge

Driving into Las Vegas at dusk
We stop talking our desert-bred
     denunciations
And gawk, the apes of amazed lust.

It's one hot-pink, neon fire
After another as the autos pulse forward,
     platelets
On the stream of talking desire.

There's no conclusion to shrewdly strike
And we love that. It's like money
     moving
From hand to shaky hand; it's like

Flesh fine as a showgirl wearing
A lace collar and nothing else or
     flaccid
As the old women fumbling in their

Suitcase-sized pocketbooks. It's
The end that doesn't end. Day and
     night
Dancing like Dantean lovers, wits

Fried in a paradise where wealth
Is gospel-shouting, testifying to
     the urge
That's a sex unto its warm self.

Fans

When Janis Joplin died,
Some people silently applauded, saying
That it went to show you can't fool around,
That she had it coming,
A bad woman, dope fiend
And that sort of world-gone-to-hell thing.
I went out back of the house and cried
Till I was spent from crying.
I lay on the October ground

But felt no peace
        and felt I never would gain peace
In this world of pursy fatalists.
My friend Raymond insisted
That white people shouldn't mix with the blues,
They couldn't handle it.

Two weeks before, Hendrix had died.
Raymond shrieked on the phone to me,
All our slang seemed like a child's uneasy bravery.

I played their records
And felt again how they turned terror into
        a good time:
He was screechingly wry, she was throbbingly kind.
Like the GIs they had told us about in school
These people died so
Others could live—
        but we could have lived if they had lived.
Enjoying yourself was not a cause or manifesto
But an attitude—goosing the gods of ordinariness,
Outraging a day-shift destiny.

If it was bad,
It was bad the way too much pathos or tequila was bad,

That blank bedrock of energy
When the singing and the sex were over
And you awoke imperfectly
To inhale a twitching cigarette,
A manager's obligations,
And the personal echo
    of those anonymous, imploring fans.

Out in the cheering dark we remain.
We are still listening but life is like death,
So strong it doesn't have to explain.

"If Vietnam is a Memory,
Then I'm a Ghost" (1980)

Toward the end he drove more than
Four hundred miles a week, never knowing
Where he was going.
The signs weren't for him.
When his wife asked where he'd been,
He'd say "Out," as if that were an answer.

Though clever people would rather not admit it,
The auto is an ambassador of freedom,
An invisible motion-cloak that lets
The mere body slice through space and banish time—
Especially at night among all those
Shimmery-bright greetings, blue and green lanterns,
Electric moons.

Soft darkness in the auto-heart as the razor of
Survival folds and sleeps.
                              Cigarette
Smoke climbs, veers, hangs, and disappears.

One night he didn't pull in around three,
The way he did each time with weird accuracy.
The end had happened already—
As dying precedes death.
She could see him fumbling with change
For a pack of smokes and looking around,
Surprised at the candy bars, loaves of bread—
The fruits of factories.

You could listen to the radio if you
Felt like it, allowing voices to be with you
That talked the deliberate, winning, sexy truth.
They knew everything important there was to know.
Though he wasn't buying it, he could listen.

He needed to forget about himself,
About his hands on the cool wheel, his legs.
It was easy to do that... sitting there.
It was easy to sit back
And absolve every last debt.

The Poverty of Theory

It's past ten-thirty, Jack's not there.
Outside the club, three low-watt bulbs feint and fizz.
She fingers her necklace—glass beads from China.
It's smooth late-spring. It's shadows.

The mind always wants more—
An unappeasable maverick,
Hungry child, avid dog,
Trickster, and cloud of metaphor.

It's almost eleven when he shows,
Heavy-eyed with a few slouching words
And brushing kiss. Still, it's okay,
Presence is nine-tenths of the law.

It's saxophone-sweet in the club,
Heaving and loose. Later
She knows it'll be even better.
She slides and dips.
You'd be a fool to refuse.

Elegy for a Detective

Bemusement was the better part of sanity,
And sanity was your glance past the surly
Occasion to the sheer morning or moment
When life relaxed and admitted all it
Wanted to do was live. "I'm happy when
The car starts and the coffee is hot," you said
And tacitly wished that our feelings would
Leave it at that. No luck—
The pirouettes of imagination never let up:
Enemies changed overnight, gunshots became
Compliments, and much-praised love was
Our most condign misunderstanding,
The hurtling of hope into the gasps of flesh.
Laconic interrogator, you smiled at all this repetition
And collected duplicates—the same childhood
Evening, the same half-confession, half-threat.
From your desk were taken the manufactures
Of what the genteel call our civilization,
A shroud of candy wrappers, lottery
Tickets, gum, sports pages,
Receipts, a hair comb, menthol cigarettes.

Death empties our little pockets;
The common usages remain silent.

If we say that we are more than
This phantasmagoria of sustenance and environment,
That our confusions yield the most unexpected fruit
And that our understanding is our best accomplice—
That is our pleasure. I think of your gentle
Contempt for humanity's evasive talkiness.
Answers mock us, back and forth we go
On a bridge of words, between
What we intend and what we forget.

History: a Conversation

Upon the demise of the Soviet Union
My breezy Republican six-figure friend Walt
Called and noted that now I wouldn't have
To indulge my "sub-existential flash-of-the-bomb fear"
Anymore.
           I could graze, as he put it,
"In slightly less-anxious pastures."
And when I reminded him that we had not yet reached
The nuclear day of Jubilee, that the guns were still loaded,
He whistled his surprisingly high-pitched,
Boy-I've-got-a-live-one whistle and said
That was true enough but the reasons to use
The "buggers" (as he offhandedly phrased it) were gone.
"We're gonna make money together. We're gonna
Divide into the two natural camps of humanity—
The fuckers and the fuckees. We're gonna run around
On airplanes and fax our specs and hustle."
Walt's energetic heaven beckoned and I sighed
My what-would-Baudelaire-have-made-
Of-the-late-twentieth-century sigh.

No more nightmares, according to Walt, and I
Want to believe him, I want to be a member of
The gouging, tie-loosed, bourbon-gulping choir.
I do. I want to believe in the effervescence
Of ignorance the way Walt does. I want to accept
The lowest common denominator as warm cash.
I don't want to worry life.

Exuberance storms through the phone.
"Bite down on the big one, kid," Walt wheezes.
And I do.

Homage to Thomas Eakins

Social rectitude hoped as always to
Correct the signs of physical reality;
More than one portrait was returned promptly—
This art of wrinkles and sagging skin
Strained the limits of moneyed grace.
The man lived in a principled whim.

Too much occurred to a face in a lifetime,
He might have protested. The years are not
Water-smooth. Even at our rest we labor.
The truth, however, went deeper than laments.
A diviner with brushes, he could predict
What is—the musculature of breath, scent of death
Like too-sweet flowers in a light-struck room.

He could accept such facts and give them praise
In all their local diversity: notable
Pose, athletic pastime, reverie, even
The surgeon's brute, dispassionate tact.

In his hometown there were no counter-salons
Or promises of bohemian paradise.
No visual crisis was present.
There were only the outskirts of clarity,
The chastising attempts to get it right.

What the age demanded was an image
Of action, the confident empire of man,
The consoling regard of the shadow female.
Marble anthems vouched for chaste perfection.

In Camden, Eakins recorded the poet Whitman—
Serenely human, at ease with tragedy.
There never was an idea equal to flesh.

The sum of all our sanctioned errands
Falls short of our vital negligence.

Bob Ward (1955)

Two nights a week Bob Ward the insurance man
Whose office stood beside the hardware store
Got in his car and drove to other rooms
In other towns to meet another man.
They loved—and held a joy that terrified
The sickly light of day. The words that seemed
To probe his every moment fell away.
The hell of every shame and fear, each nod
And smile, the famous business handshake
Unplumed in the cock's hard grace. He prayed
For himself later in the clock-bound dark.
He prayed for the soul that seemed unreal
But must be there. He cried peculiar tears
And watched the sun come up: the slightest pink
Flame simmered on the horizon. He chose a tie
To match his suit then headed to the cafe
Where each morning he took his determined place.

Farmers Go Crazy Slowly

"Farmers go crazy slowly," the mental health man
    Says and pauses.
      The crowd guffaws or tries to,
Knowing that there is some truth
      There, that a farmer walks
Too many steps to ever get into a hurry.

They want him to say that it is okay to keep
      Going on, that
        No one will bother them.
They want to hear some lies, the way
Everyone else gets to hear some lies.

The January night is still and puzzling
      As a dead machine.
        It is a pitiful time
Of year, a time to lose your courage
Or look for the golden age when work
      Made everything go.
Brilliance did not matter then, a pair
Of hard red hands was clever enough.

Once you have the answer, you don't need answers,
      Understanding, for instance, that
        Not much occurs in a day,
A cow might die but a calf will thrive,
      Understanding that the land abides—
Acreage, wilderness, garden, barnyard, and grave.

Farmers go crazy slowly, trying to grasp
What debt has to do with devotion.
      In the mail another numbered notice.
      In the frozen fields three crows.
Working is a bridle and a bit, but the way
The crows cackle, there could be a party.

It is so damn cold.
This parcel of blood could sit and cackle with pleasure,
Like a crazy man at a party.

Housing Project

Something new, once, under the pale
Northern sun, this stooping, squalid height
Immobilizes the most prescient optimist's eye.
JoJo shoots hoops but lacks the size.
Everyone who isn't a rectangle has a problem.

On the other side of the world, Wojtek K.
Bounces a ball down the dreariest of dreary halls,
Headfakes a door and alley-oops off the wall.
Nobody could live here, but people offer
Bribes to the janitors who sit through the long,
Slow mornings and ponder the meaning of schnapps.

Jésus goes in for a lay-up but his chances
Of making the pros are strictly metaphysical.
Rational fraternity was never his thing.
He passes off inexplicably. The easy moves
Bore him. His instincts are his fame.

Everywhere the game remains the same:
One team has papers and the power
To make people grateful for the chance
To rent a subsidized grave;
The other team shouts and puts the ball
Through the rim at twenty feet,
Their bodies rising like dolphins into
The imperfection of dreams.

Delmore Schwartz

Within one human being the fifty-seven
Varieties of bedevilment
Coexisted incautiously, eager
To salt, infect, and leaven poem, story,
Essay, or letter with a modernist
Elizabethan college-cafeteria rhetoric.
He was present the way children hold their hands
Up to indicate that yes they are there,
Ready, in this case, to dun the muse,
Practice the arts of self-promotion,
Flatter the damnable world, be damned one's self
In an operatic yet colloquial fashion:
One day Hal, the next Antony—
All the while trying to make stretched ends meet,
All the while dabbling in coterie civilities,
All the while diving into seductive buoyancies.
He could hear Eliot discreetly brooding
Across the ocean; he could smell the competition—
A bucolic waft up through a subway grate
And on into the airplane-ridden empyrean.

A poet is an unsuitable joke able
To mimic any legend of the past thousand years.
A poet's heart is a well that has
No Apollonian bottom—and a modern heart
At that, looking backwards when no one is looking,
Promulgating its inventive energy,
Searching out the cabals of grown-up boys' clubs,
Lubricating the influence of
A horse-playing uncle who knows a cop who knows
A judge who can get you into the *Anglican-
Cum-Jewish Panfried New Critical Review.*

Souls clap hands in the Hollywood night.
Get-rich schemes grow like mushrooms in Poland.

Let's call up Shakespeare. What would he say?
The receiver sits in your wieldy hands.
Someone is going to reply to
The vaudevillian vicar's summary of
The last days of eternity: cakes and despair
In the cozy purlieus of East Coca-Cola.
Someone is going to reply.
In the meantime, poet, wait.

At the Lincoln Memorial

Young couples with sticky, squalling children
    Try to revive
Memories of chapter twenty-three:
    Quiz tomorrow.
A group of South American sailors takes
    Pictures quietly.
Ice-cream wrappers swirl down the many steps,
    People caress
Their aching feet. And everyone has questions:
    What does the government
Do about the pigeons? Where are the restrooms? How
    Many tons of stone?
Still hot in the late afternoon, there seems to be
    No history today.
Off by the 'Nam Wall someone is down on
    The ground moaning.
An older man. Attempted lectures sputter,
    The high ground
Of certitude offers distended views,
    The traffic whines.
Baffled pride rejects, nonetheless, the dying fall.
    Memory's seeds
Root like the weeds between the cracks.

Sister Angela (1947)

The sad, flat light of midwinter
Afternoon softly tints the varnished desks.

It is still and she relishes each mote
Of time. It was so long ago when she

Herself was a brat with pigtails
And muslin dress. Each day

She feels the passing miracle of children
Though she'd never been one for softness:

When a child held out a hand
The wooden ruler came down hard.

The pain was real—but so was
The forgiveness. It's that, she thinks,

That she offers—out of the boisterous muddle
Of feeling a glimmer of discipline,

Of the accuracy it takes to find
And hold onto God the other six days.

A chore of sorts—ungrand, unspecial.
You could die inside such a regimen.

You could die inside this amber classroom,
Inside the frail pages of books.

She knew that and looked hard
Into each child's wild face

To feel not so much the sweet courtesy
As the blind heart that her savior

Had known and touched
And still died for.

(for Christopher Corkery)

The Beltway

To hypostatize the moody hodgepodge of auto-
Reverie requires another pedal—
The turbo overhead one-ton metaphysic.
Mindfully I hammer that sucker while
A tan Bonneville zips by and the woman at
The wheel wears a deep-set smile as if she
Just got sincerely laid or was thinking
About her favorite flower—peonies delirous
With petals—or remembering something calmly
Serious one of her children said, something provoked
By life's quivering uncertainty that only a child
Could say. The exaggerated respect that the Romantics
Paid to children wasn't totally misplaced.
Anyone knows that adults are too hectic
For both their real and hypothetical good.

I like to think that someday I'll sit down with
These whizzing people and ask each one
About where we come from and where we are going.
At the moment I turn on a radio talk show where
Some guy is in a fever about the Bullets' lack
Of a point guard who can dish and penetrate.
The Bullets! What about the sweethearts, the rainbows,
The jump apostles, the babycakes?

If automobiles are cocoons then each time
We step out we are bright as a new butterfly
Greeting the huge, shifting air and the hum
Of the ambient ten thousand things. It's at
That first moment or so of the feet on the ground—
The inverse of the insect's initial flutter—
That I want to grip and keep with me all
The time because it's then that I recall the earth
And my legs and I feel so transparently solid,
So animate because I can stand and walk.

Weather

They were in an old-time, thin-wood orange crate
Held barely together with fencewire and according
To the lawyer who handled Raymond's estate
They were a bequest to us. Raymond wrote
(And we actually saw his own upright script)
That we would know what to do with them.

And what did that mean? That we were
Out-of-staters, hence romantics, incompetents,
But incurably human as we hung around Ray's
Kitchen in the gloom of a late November afternoon
And listened passionately as Ray told story
After offhand story—a few about death
But most about the peculiarities of life.
Ray hated characters, those who confused
Personality with content. In his white-church, dry-beans,
Backyard-violets way, Ray hated excess.
"There's a point to that," Ray would mumble
In his gnarled, phlegmy voice, "there's a point,"
Though he never enunciated even once his intent.

He wanted us to hear how it had been
And we wanted to learn. I don't think we
Ever neared affection for each other.
Ray's wife had died of cancer before we came
To Blair County; his son had gone down
In a transport off New Guinea in '44.
Ray sold off his herd, cut pulp off his
Couple of hundred acres and avoided debts.
"I want to die clear," he liked to say.

"Poetry," you said teasingly as we opened
The crate top and they were journal books,
Those sturdy, marbled-cover kind with ruled pages.
There had to be a couple of dozen of them.

We tentatively, ostentatiously began
Reading aloud. We were afraid and we wanted
To share whatever unhappy surprise
Might be lurking. We didn't want to discover
Anything separately. It had to be shared.

It was weather! Notebooks filled with frosts,
Air temperatures, fogs, hay, snows,
Written in pencil, fountain, and ballpoint pen
And each date bearing the day of the week.
A line or two of observation and information
Sufficed for all times of the year. He played no favorites.

I hunted for words—an adjective that trembled
Or glinted, a noun that had the black authority
Of deep, incontrovertible feeling—but nothing,
Only carefully serviceable phrases—"hot enough
To fry an egg," "southwind," "light snow at dusk,"
"Mud almost up to the top of my boots."

We stopped reciting to one another, instead reading
To ourselves silently, seated in our kitchen
On a March afternoon, one of those nondescript
Sunshine and clouds, late winter days.
When we looked up and locked eyes, we both
Nodded spontaneously. We didn't cry or clap.
We knew that we'd been trusted with something
Truer than common. Ray didn't want words.
The feeling of being present each day was—
When you got right down to it—lordly.

The Economy

Sometimes he forgot that anyone
Was down there.
Forty floors did that—
The windows sealed and tinted,
The ventilators humming and trilling,
The weather removed.

As a heaven
It was not so much godlike or compassionate
As it was numerical, the playground
Of percentage points and analyses,
Of tall columns of unstartled figures.
You got lost in it.
It made perfect sense.
You outwitted people you'd never see.

Somedays he can see the dwarfed steeples
Of stone churches, their determined magnificence
Turned homely.
During the week they're like museums,
Open for informative tours and gazing.

He remembers his mother walking
Onto their porch one rainy winter day
And there was a man crouched in
The corner of the porch like a rabbit
Or a dog.
His mother's screams were red
Bullets and the man bolted down the steps,
Across the yard, arms flailing.

On the street corner there's a man with
Matted hair and lost eyes. It takes him
Five fumbled seconds to mouth, "Spare change?"
Seeing him is painful, giving him a quarter

Is painful, not giving him a quarter is painful.
The drama of coins is hopelessly finite;
The weariness of suffering is dumbfounding.
Today, however, the stockbroker isn't addressed
And walks on. But there's
Tomorrow and the day after tomorrow.

We've abandoned eternity, the broker thinks
Almost absent-mindedly,
Halfway down the next block. The word sits
In his head, plausible yet distant as a cloud.
He stops and looks into a shop window that holds
Many neatly folded dress shirts. Two for
Eighty-two. He sees himself in the glowing glass,
A man on ground level, someone who is visible
But who—across these precise distances—can't be heard.

Fast Food Incident

Actually it's in McDonald's—one place in this world
Everybody's been—but it could have been some similarly
Brisk eatery. Steve's ordered two cheeseburgers
(Not a double, two separate ones, please) and he
Separates the syllables in "separate" until they're
Distant cousins in different time zones. Also a Coke,
Though it could have been a Pepsi. He's touchy
That way too, the whole Coke Pepsi thing.

When he gets the plastic-wrapped food he takes the cover
Off and says that there's no blood, that he can't
Eat flesh unless there's some blood, that he needs
To know he's eating a creature who once also roamed
The perishable earth. He can't eat a fraction
Or a symbol or a placebo. The high school kid behind
The counter takes two staggering steps backwards
Like she's been popped in the gut and I'm thinking
Shit he hasn't taken his tranquilization medication
The clockwork blueblack horse that rides away with him
And I say that's a real arty thing to say
And I wait but not long because Steve's loopiest
Dearest smile starts to emerge. Art, he gurgles,
Blood's not art. Blood's not even a pretty shade of red.
But we're not the only people there—that's the beauty
Of life—and some popeye of a guy in a tee shirt
All ropey muscles and a voice like a hernia
Says I'll take 'em off your hands buddy.

Generosity, Steve says as he takes his first wolfish
Bite as we move to our booth and it's okay to
Look around again like regular people with a couple
Of grievances but not looking for a fight.

Squares

"No sweet way," Johnny used to say
In that high-as-a-March-kite voice
While flinging one hand away in a gesture
Of quick, Bette Davis contempt.
He'd read some Jean Genet
And seated at the bar in those tight, black,
"Continental" pants
And plain, cleanwhite shirt,
He'd invoke his cock as both the law and the crime.
"I live by it and for it
But if you're not desperate you're not
Living anyhow," and he'd pause for effect
Throw his head back and laugh
An ingratiating but hungry laugh.
Tossed out of the house at sixteen
He could back up every word with a story
And some stories with scars.
"They're squares. You know, husbands
And accountants and civic leaders.
Guys who read the newspaper and take it
Seriously like the world rested on their fucking shoulders.
They want it so bad.
They whimper like babies.
I love them then. I mean it's sort of pure.
They're so gone then—they'd do anything.
Not that I'm one to take advantage
Of a sex-starved banker," and he'd
Smile a happy, sly, electric smile.

It wasn't a jazzman's bar, but that late—
Thanks to payoffs and handouts—it was
An open bar and the musicians would be there
Talking and making plans for the rest of the evening.
"Christ, I wish I had an ear," Johnny would say
And the guys would look at him in a weirdly

Respectful way as if he could do
What they did but just wasn't choosing to do it.

"Endings are always sordid,"
And Johnny's was in that category,
Somewhere between jealousy—"how tacky"—
And larceny—"how common."

"Hell's farther uptown," he'd say
And posture slightly.
"And heaven is right here."

Dying in the Hospital

His daughter babbles on about some
Social incident: what she said, what

Someone else said, what she said.
Distant as he is, he tries to listen.

His son stares moodily at the vase of Shasta daisies.
Coarse but unflagging flowers, a gift from the office.

Die already. He knows his children think it
And he wishes he could oblige.

He needs a tattoo that says Science Owns My Body.
The laboratories and engines of the late century

Keep pulling him back, reassembling him.
The technology of humanism isn't human.

The dragon of pain roars
And the man disappears in the fog of medication.

Still, he is supposed to be affable, charitable.
And why complain to the nurses who work

For twelve hours straight and look at him
With fatigued compassion, boredom, and purposefulness?

A job to do. He always thought that way too.
Everyone does—admit it or not.

This is it, but as the bare trees outside
The window and the scuffle of shoes

In the hall perseveringly indicate
This was always it.

The Copper-Colored Stain

The walls are thin as sheets and the boarder
Next door snores, a groaning nose-bellow.
In the morning the snorer is ruddy, fresh
And cheerful. K. is unable to get used
To this nightly concert and loses on the average
An hour's sleep listening to sounds that have
Been likened in the newspapers to Schoenberg's music.

There is no line before the bathroom door.
Each person knows his time and acts accordingly.
Watches and clocks are a blessing.
The copper-colored stain in the sink never varies.
It's the water, even though the water is clear,
The chemist's assistant avers that it's the water.

Mrs. Prokopka, the widow who keeps
This establishment, reveres the king, the Pope
And her pet rabbit, a glutton named Oscar.
The rabbit nips any finger that comes near him
That does not hold a morsel of food.
The rabbit sniffles and winces at who knows what?
All the lodgers try to stay in the good graces
Of the rabbit who according to Mrs. Prokopka
Is "wise, humorous, and cavalier."

K. generally listens to everything that is said
To him although at the end of a clerk's long day
He could not repeat every remark. Every remark
Isn't worth remembering in any case although
Some stay embedded in one's mind like arrowheads
And not necessarily the most pertinent remarks.

Whenever a boarder has visited the red-light district
Mrs. Prokopka makes a small scene about some

Insignificant thing the next morning. How does she know?
Thus, life is a succession of small scenes.

Erlaub, the hotel clerk, blames the world's
Troubles on the Jews.
Hassenfuss, the tram conductor, blames the world's
Troubles on the Swiss: "They are so secretive."
Gottschalk, a pastor without a church, blames
The world's troubles on infidels.
Everyone at the table nods but disagrees
As to the specifics. Good-naturedly they quarrel.

When it snows K. is happy although he cannot
Say why it should be so as he detests wearing rubber
Overshoes. Still, the sight of the falling "flakes,"
As people call them, lightens and cheers him
As if he were once again a breathless child.

(for Howard Levy)

Kissing

Under a pale, pastel, early morning sky,
    webbed indigos and gray-yellows,
Hannah Grebholzer and Harry Fox
    exchanged succulent, yielding kisses.

Necks extended forward, flamingo-like,
    they clutched trig and French books,
While all their teenage being
    simmered in their supple, grappling mouths.

The bus driver we called Ajax—
    a tallow face tattooed with stubble—
Asked aloud if love wasn't grand.
    He rat-a-tatted his fingers on the wheel

And hummed a concoction he called swing.
    Minutes elapsed that were more
Than millennia. Oh kisses were overripe apples;
    fondled scents; plush instincts

Of the warm, exhaling earth; exclamatory
    sighs distended into weak-kneed moans,
As if mortals balanced the maculate tension
    of passion like a globe that is still, and spins.

My Wife Asks Me Why I Keep Photographs in a Drawer

Beneath tee shirts and underwear
A few almost-sepia photographs
Of my mother and father—before they knew me.

My mother stands in front of the school
Where she first taught fourth grade.
She's young and lovely and smiling
In a summer dress. Her shoulders are bare,
Her eyes alight with candid feeling.
The year before she worked in
A department store where she read Tolstoy
During her breaks. One day she came back
To her counter red-eyed; her supervisor inquired
About her. "Anna died," my mother blurted.

My father sits at a table. He holds some cards
And smiles. All the other guys at the table
Are soldiers too and they smile. They're going
To live through the war. It's aces and swell
Broads and highballs and home runs for them.

I should set up some sort of shrine for these
Bouquets of time, something more visible. They
Lie there in my drawer as I stutter through
My slice of time—from semi-hippiedom
To that middle-age wariness
That signals a flagging of mortal belief.

I never take them out. I know them too well.
It's dark in the drawer and common and hidden.
Photos tell you that people can smile at
The dark eye of oblivion. Albums and walls are
Too insistent. What's part of every fumbling
Morning is closer to the fleeting mark.

Hettie Smith

When Hettie Smith our maid would quit, she'd tell
My mother that as an employer she was
"Unfeeling, unclean, and unholy." My mother would
Start to blubber and protest her love and if
I was there I wondered who was holy
In this sweaty world. A few days later
Hettie would return quietly and life went on.

Hettie told me that white people thought they
Knew so much about colored people but they didn't.
In fact white folks were simple as infants.
"You imagine a grown man in a diaper—that's
A white man. Colored folks are here to sanctify
The world. It says so in the Bible," Hettie said.
I'd read Bertrand Russell and told her the Bible
Was a lie. She turned around and slapped me
As deftly as a cat swats a mouse. I was fourteen
And sputtered indignantly. "The Lord have mercy
On you," she intoned prayerfully. "The Lord have mercy."

One sweltering day she had a stroke on the number
Four streetcar. She died right there.
At her funeral her son Lawrence got up and said
That we were exploiters and devils. It was the 60s.
I bit my lip and looked around warily
As if I had blinders on or dark glasses.
Emmeline, Hettie's oldest daughter, rose up
And said that there was no place for hate on this day,
That hate dried up the rivers of our hearts.
Years later Lawrence sent us a brief letter.
We weren't evil, he wrote, just well-meaning.

I think of all the judgments we make
About starching shirts and wiping tables
And cooking a pot roast and taking an aspirin,

How we grind each day on the lathe of experience
And marvel at the unappeasable friction,
And I think of Hettie's slap, her flower-print dresses,
The petite mole on her right cheek and her faith
That was as approachable as it was strong.

Rent

The sun is fire.
I drive a car
While Mister Gelb
Collects his rents.

17 to his 72
I listen to his stories
About *schvartzers,*
Robberies, murders

While playing one
Of the Negro radio
Stations down low.
From the car I see faces

This calmly infernal
Day as they hand
Over 12 dollars,
14, 16.

The small cloth bag
Lies between us
And at one row
House missing its

Screen door Mister
Gelb stands talking
Forever with a tall
Bony woman

As slowly a man
Approaches our car
And says to me
Very distinctly,

"I know what you got
And I don't want it."
He leaves as Mister
Gelb returns.

I turn the key
As I hear the old man
Berate this life
Which disfigures our years.

Strangers

Around the time of the month
In the warm weather
When there was no or little moon
My mother's voice would assume
An unusual urgency.
"We need to drive beyond the lights,"
She'd say as she searched
For her customarily misplaced keys.

My sister and I got into
The two-tone Ford Fairlane
And after a half-hour we
Had left incipient suburbia
Behind. My mother's driving-
The-car-humming had settled into

A modest soprano that
Wandered through the Hit Parade
Of 1941, now brassy,
Now wistful, now jaunty.

She pulled over on some
Dirt road and we got out.
The air was rich and spectral.
You could smell the fields, cows,
Soil, woods. We walked
Carefully, pausing now and then
To look up at the stars
Whose names we didn't know.
We were city people and they
Were amazing strangers.

We marveled and my sister and I
Sang along as best we could.
No houses or stores or streetlights.

It was dark in the country and
It felt buoyantly and quietly right.

Death of a Woodcutter (1954)

He watched himself begin to fall—
A gradual twitch,
Blood in a filthy kerchief.

A man who rose
Each morning to acid coffee
Taken at an empty table

In no light and near light,
His pulpy hands were engines,
His mind a bemused witness.

For near forever he'd measured
The hound of work, its bark
And feckless bite, its rubbing up

Against the legs of whistling days,
Its steps through the endless woods
At once deliberate and dreamy.

The family of empty bottles
And the kennel of strays
Neither mourned nor cheered

A hermit's aching grandeur. The man
In question neither crabbed nor prayed
But traced the force of wood—

The hard swelling, the grace
Of green iron—
And the saw's modern noise

Like nothing heard before:
The moment biting long years,
The devil's pragmatic roar.

Shoplifting

The store dick lays a hand on your shoulder
Three steps from the exit. He asks what's
In your pockets but it's more like a statement
Than a question. Two candy bars and a roll of film.

Your stomach melts and your heart starts to beat
Like when you used to race on the playground.
He tells you to sit down on the bench by the doors.
Usually there are some old people sitting there

Gabbling about bargains but no one's around
This late in the evening. You expect the manager
To show up and give you a lecture about kids
Nowadays but he doesn't

And when the cop appears he doesn't say
Anything special beyond you'll have to go to court.
When he gives you the paper he's almost smiling
Or he's not there at all, he's not seeing you.

Thoughts, thoughts... your head's raw dough
One moment, light as a balloon the next.
They're always playing a song in the background
In these stores that you can't quite identify.

Your foot's tapping to the vacant beat
And after the cop leaves and you
Can leave you don't for some minutes.
You don't even own a camera.

1978

A couple of years after the bicentennial
Once the fire of self-congratulation had simmered down
To the normal frenzy of electro-Jeffersonian desire
We headed west in one of my younger brother's three Fords—
Uninsured and fast. Officially and unofficially
The Nuclear Bullet Tour: that's why we went,
Leaving the comfortably filthy streets, airshafts
And ethnic snacks of Brooklyn behind,
The human grid of orderly transience, to sniff out
Missile silos, the long knife in America's back pocket,
To go underground as Dante did once upon a time
Even though he did it in a book.
Not being in a book, we figured we could go him
One better, get a look at the control panels of Dis,
A brightly-lit, well-ventilated place
Part-Hollywood, part mannish hypno-tech.

Meanwhile canyons, rivers and mountains, majesty
That makes words evaporate, millions of years
And the god who dwarfs our feeble Sundays.
We drank a good-sized farm pond worth of coffee,
Kept earnest poetic journals that make me want
To cry now when I read them: the sunrises outside
Of Nowhere, glinting breezes (I wanted to say "zephyrs"),
The half-inch of dew, we just lying there
In sleeping bags, warm and waiting for the sky.

Outside Omaha a cop pulled us over
For a dead taillight. No ticket or hassle,
Your where-you-boys-from sort of cop.
The closest we got to the beast was a checkpoint
In North Dakota. We said we were taxpayers
And the guard smiled about three teeth's worth of a smile.
"Who are you assholes kidding?" he said.
Hard to argue with him.

I guess we thought the earth would open up somehow.
We chanted over the 327, "Nuke Spook, Nuke Spook."

"Those bombs help people, they never gonna be used,"
An old-timer told us one morning in a cafe in Montana.
"You boys got yourselves all worked up about nothin'.
Only a fool would fuck this place up." And he gestured with
The stump of an arm he retained from WWII.
He took us to his ranch where we spent a few days
Moseying around on horses so intelligent and calm
Even we could ride them.
                              When we saw Chicago
We stopped in a bar on the outskirts, one of those
Near-cities not-towns and bought a round of drinks
For the four people in there at two o'clock on a gray
Afternoon. "To hell," we said. No one demurred.

Allegory

Happiness comes over to the house
    and brings her friends with her
    in her big Chev station wagon.
    It needs new shocks. The paint job
    is called, "Spring Blue."

Alacrity licks all the crumbs off her plate
    and applauds the electric lights.
Pleasure strokes the cat.
Contentment hums show tunes and watches
    the dust settle.
Orgasm is unruly.
Civility murmurs assent.
Gaiety does handstands and paints her toenails.
Sanguine deftly unfolds the hopes of the new administration.
    Democracy is messy but better than
    anything else, she avers.
Savor kisses the condiments, particularly the relishes.

When they leave, I go out to buy a newspaper.
I'm whistling some Duke Ellington and I've got on
    my soft, worn, corduroy baseball cap.
The guy who gives me change with my Lifesavers and
    lottery ticket asks me what's up.
Joy, I say. I love her. She's berserk.

For Pleasure (Bob Corin's Pickup)

I'm driving in my pickup which is a Ford
Because Ford built America and I respect that
Though the Pilgrims were go-getters too, coming over
Here in those little wooden boats they had to be crazy
Or believers like the Four Square Gospel people or both
And Karen's with me right up snug against me.
I hate it when you look in a truck and there's air
Between a man and a woman, she's sitting at one end
Thinking about a refrigerator and he's at the other
End thinking about bird hunting and that's
All their lives are is their damn thoughts.
I'm trying to get a song on the radio but I'm
Getting the news which is about some Russians
And the White House, although it's their White House
Not ours. They're fighting of course.
Karen wants a Softserve at the Dairy Delite
Which is good with me because I like to see her tongue
Go dabbling in that sweet stuff. You can't beat
A tongue for pleasure. It must have been hell
When they used to cut people's tongues out.
I'd rather go blind. Now it's
The Stock Market which I could give a shit about.
The only person I knew who cared about that
Was Billy Thompson the lawyer's son who was
The only boy in the French Club in high school
And it wasn't on account of the girls.
He liked French. Which is sort of sad to my mind.
Anyhow I put my money into my truck. It's got
Chrome-plated tailpipes and a set of mudflaps
With Yosemite Sam on them saying, "Back Off!"
That sort of shit.
I start to mash the gas pedal down because I'd like
To drive right out of this poem but I can't of course.
I'm like one of those clowns that Shakespeare
Liked to make fun of, though clown

Doesn't mean make-up and a red nose like at
The Shrine circus. It means a rustic, someone
Who prefers living to talking about living.
Writers fear life so they make art. Which
Is cozy and I can't blame them. Karen's burning
A hole in my thigh. She's rubbing her thigh against
Mine kind of distracted-like and I'd just as soon
Stay with her in this rapid box until next week.
I'm not credible, I'm not predictable, I'm not malleable.
I wish I could eat every word in Karen's spacious mouth.

Voice: the Entertainer

I'm fifty-two years of age which means
My shirt has a hard time covering my gut
And under my chin and jaw the skin's starting
To hang like a wet washcloth and I'm singing
About love.
There was a time and a place when that word
Had something to say to my life but it's
Been awhile, it's been awhile.

Still, there's something called divorce out there
And the crowd—from around thirty-five to the early
Fifties—likes the oldies, likes the safety
And slow ecstasy of the past.
As do I. The songs stay young although
The people don't and I like it when I look
Out over the dance floor which could be in a bar
Or a gym or an armory or some godforsaken hall

Built in the last century for farmers or preachers
And I see the couples close to each other, the women
Sort of resting themselves against the men and the men
Sort of tight but trying to relax and the sex urge
Going back and forth between them like an electric charge.
I like that because it's formal but it's human,
I like that because people don't get to dance much,
They're busy being beauticians and teachers and contractors.

It's Sock Hop Night or Golden Memories
And I'm down on my creaky knees singing that
When I lost my baby I almost lost my mind
And the sax player who's half my age and tokes up
Before each show even though I tell him I don't
Want him messed up on the stage, is really moaning,
A righteous kid, and I know I'm telling people
The truth, the funky but pure truth.

A Quiet Life

What a person desires in life
   is a properly boiled egg.
This isn't as easy as it seems.
There must be gas and a stove,
     the gas requires pipelines, mastodon drills,
     banks that dispense the lozenge of capital.
There must be a pot, the product of mines
    and furnaces and factories,
     of dim early mornings and night-owl shifts,
     of women in kerchiefs and men with
    sweat-soaked hair.
Then water, the stuff of clouds and skies
    and God knows what causes it to happen.
There seems always too much or too little
    of it and more pipelines, meters, pumping
    stations, towers, tanks.
And salt—a miracle of the first order,
    the ace in any argument for God.
    Only God could have imagined from
    nothingness the pang of salt.
Political peace too. It should be quiet
    when one eats an egg. No political hoodlums
    knocking down doors, no lieutenants who are
    ticked off at their scheming girlfriends and
    take it out on you, no dictators
    posing as tribunes.
It should be quiet, so quiet you can hear
    the chicken, a creature usually mocked as a type
    of fool, a cluck chained to the chore of her body.
Listen, she is there, pecking at a bit of grain
    that came from nowhere.

Acknowledgments

The following poems have appeared previously or have been accepted for publication:

The Paris Review: "Listening to a Baseball Game"; "Somerset County"; "Elegy for a Detective"; "On the Bus to Houston"; "Shoplifting"

New England Review: "Dramatis Personae (1957)"; "It's a Party (1959)"; "Fans"; "Weather"; "Squares"

The Manhattan Review: "1978"; "Rudinsky's, 1953"; "A Quiet Life"; "Homage to Thomas Eakins"; "Delmore Schwartz"; "Mark Rothko, 1903–1970"; "Comics"; "Who St. Augustine Was"; "Fast Food Incident"

River Styx: "Sonnet"

Poetry: "American Poem of the Senior Citizenry"; "The Poverty of Theory"

Denver Review: "Young Ahab"; "For D.R., Dead of AIDS at Age 25"; "Simon Turetzky Who Died at Dachau"

Beloit Poetry Journal: "Tricia LeClair"; "Cow Symphony"

The New Yorker: "Swayed"

Long Shot: "History: a Conversation"

Sewanee Review: "Vegas: the Urge"; "Diary of an Ant"

Embers: "Farmers Go Crazy Slowly"

Poetry East: "Housing Project"

Crazyhorse: "Kissing"; "Dying in the Hospital"

The Virginia Quarterly Review: "The Beltway"; "Single-Life Blues"

The Illinois Review: "If Vietnam is a Memory, Then I'm a Ghost (1980)"; "Death of a Woodcutter"

The Quotable Moose: "Bob Ward (1955)"

Tampa Review: "At the Lincoln Memorial"; "Poems"

Northwest Review: "Sister Angela (1947)"

Ontario Review: "Children's Ward"; "Beethoven's Maid"; "Rent"

Graham House Review: "Pikesville"

Southwest Review: "The Economy"

The Southern Review: "Hettie Smith"; "Voice: the Entertainer"

The North Stone Review: "Allegory"; "Strangers"

The Kenyon Review: "My Wife Asks Me Why I Keep Photographs in a Drawer"

Mid-American Review: "For Pleasure (Bob Corin's Pickup)"

"Fans" was reprinted in *Sweet Nothings: An Anthology of Rock and Roll in American Poetry;* "Somerset County" was reprinted in *The Quotable Moose.*

The Author

Baron Wormser is the author of three previous collections of poetry: *The White Words* (Houghton Mifflin, 1983), *Good Trembling* (Houghton Mifflin, 1985), and *Atoms, Soul Music, and Other Poems* (Paris Review Editions, 1989). His poems, essays, and reviews have appeared in a wide variety of journals including *The Paris Review, Sewanee Review, The New Republic, Harper's,* and *Poetry.* He was born and raised in Baltimore, Maryland,

Maisie Wormser

and has lived since 1971 in Maine where he has worked as a librarian. He has taught at the University of Maine at Farmington and at the Robert Frost Place.